Created, published, and distributed by Knock Knock
1635-B Electric Ave.
Venice, CA 90291
knockknockstuff.com
Knock Knock is a registered trademark of Knock Knock LLC

Printed in China

ISBN: 978-160106829-3
UPC: 825703-50158-2

10 9 8 7 6 5 4 3 2 1

This Is a Fucking Quote Book

KNOCK KNOCK®
VENICE, CALIFORNIA

This book is dedicated to the eminent individuals whose words are parodied herein. We'd like to imagine each of them, living or dead, getting a chuckle out of it. We only wish we could invite them all to dinner. That would be a great fucking party.

Houston, Tranquility Base here. The Eagle has **fucking** landed.

—Neil Armstrong

Trust yourself. You know more than you fucking think you do.

—Dr. Benjamin Spock

Use the fucking force, Luke.

—Obi Wan-Kenobi, *Star Wars*

You get a fucki
you get a fucki
you get a fucki
Everybody gets

—Oprah Winfrey

g car,
g car,
g car!
a fucking car!

If you are always trying to be normal, you will never know how fucking amazing you can be.

—Maya Angelou

Two roads diverged in
a wood, and I—

I took the one less traveled by,

And that has made all the
fucking difference.

—Robert Frost

Anything that the
women of this country
fucking want, I want
to fucking give them.

—Theodore Roosevelt

Christmas won't be Christmas without any fucking presents.

—Louisa May Alcott

This above all:
to thine own fucking
self be true.

—William Shakespeare

Don't stop be-fuckin'-lievin'.

—Journey

A man hath no better thing under the sun, than to fucking eat, and to fucking drink, and to fucking be merry.

—Ecclesiastes 8:15

I've got a fever.
And the only
prescription is more
fucking cowbell.

—Christopher Walken, *Saturday Night Live*

Oh, good fucking grief!

—Charlie Brown

I am woman, hear me fucking roar.

—Helen Reddy

Government of the fucking people, by the fucking people, for the fucking people.

—Abraham Lincoln

And that's the way it fucking is.

—Walter Cronkite

The person, be it
gentleman or lady,
who has not pleasure
in a good novel,
must be intolerably
fucking stupid.

—Jane Austen

Do you believe in fucking miracles?

—Al Michaels

I am the fucking

—Muhammad Ali

greatest.

In the midst of winter
I finally learned
that there was
in me an invincible
fucking summer.

—Albert Camus

Any discrimination based
simply on race or color
is fucking barbarous.

—W. E. B. DuBois

I want to sing like
birds sing, not
worrying about
who the fuck hears,
or what the fuck
they think.

—Rumi

I can’t believe I ate
the whole fuckin’ thing.

—Alka Seltzer

Life is either
a daring fucking
adventure
or nothing.

—Helen Keller

I am free of
all prejudices.
I fucking hate
everyone
equally.

—W. C. Fields

Carry your chin in
and the crown of your
head high. We are gods
in the fucking chrysalis.

—Dale Carnegie

E.T. fuckin' phone home.

—E.T., *E.T. the Extra-Terrestrial*

We've got a really big fucking show.

—Ed Sullivan

The only thing we have to fucking fear is fucking fear itself.

—Franklin D. Roosevelt

Do. Or do not.
There is no
fucking try.

—Yoda, *The Empire Strikes Back*

Mr. Gorbachev, tear down this fucking wall.

—Ronald Reagan

Equal fucking pay for equal fucking work.

—Susan B. Anthony

War is fucking hell.

—Napoleon Bonaparte

The ultimate measure
he stands in moments
convenience, but wher
fucking challenge and

—Dr. Martin Luther King, Jr.

a man is not where
fucking comfort and
ie stands at times of
ntroversy.

A difference in taste in jokes is a great fucking strain on the affections.

—George Eliot

I do not like them
Sam-I-am.
I do not fuckin' like
green eggs and ham.

—Dr. Seuss

Just fuckin' do it.

—Nike

And they were both naked,
the man and his wife, and
were not fucking ashamed.

—Genesis 2:25

Sometimes a cigar
is just a fucking cigar.

—Sigmund Freud

If you retain nothing else, always remember the most important Rule of Beauty. "Who the fuck cares?"

—Tina Fey

There are and there will be thousands of princes. There is only one fucking Beethoven.

—Ludwig van Beethoven

I shot the fucking sheriff.

—Bob Marley

Immature poets imitate; mature poets fucking steal.

—T. S. Eliot

Bah, fucking Humbug!

—Charles Dickens

A thousand-mile journey
Begins with a single fucking step.

—Lao Tzu

Wax the fuck on,
wax the fuck off.

—Mr. Miyagi, *The Karate Kid*

Yes is a
fucking world.

—e. e. cummings

I fucking love my fucking self.

—Kendrick Lamar

Drama is very
in life: you hav
on with a fuck

—Julia Child

nportant
to come
g bang.

A little learning
is a dang'rous
fuckin' thing.

—Alexander Pope

I am the fucking Alpha and Omega.

—Revelation 1:8

Where there is great fucking love there are always miracles.

—Willa Cather

All I know
is I'm not
a fucking
Marxist.

—Karl Marx

You must fucking do the thing you think you cannot fucking do.

—Eleanor Roosevelt

We are not fucking amused.

—Queen Victoria

Stay me with flagons,
comfort me with
apples: for I am sick
the fuck of love.

—Song of Solomon 2:5

Wine [is] constant proof that God loves us and loves to see us **fucking** happy.

—Benjamin Franklin

I wish that every
human life might
be pure transparent
fucking freedom.

—Simone de Beauvoir

Of course I know how to roll a fucking joint.

—Martha Stewart

It is better to
light one candle
than to curse the
fucking darkness.

—Motto of The Christophers

They're
magically
fucking
delicious.

—Lucky Charms

Posterity! You will never know, how much it cost the present Generation, to preserve your fucking Freedom! I hope you will make a good fucking Use of it.

—John Adams

This is fucking America and I am allowed to have healthy fucking self-esteem.

—Amy Poehler

In the field of public educ
"separate but equal" has
educational facilities are

—US Supreme Court Chief Justice Earl Warren, *Brown v.*

on the doctrine of
fucking place. Separate
erently fucking unequal.

of Education

Senator, you're no fucking Jack Kennedy.

—Lloyd Bentsen

You're gonna need
a bigger fucking boat.

—Martin Brody, *Jaws*

Let other pens dwell
the fuck on fucking
guilt and misery.

—Jane Austen

No, I do not weep at the fucking world—I am too busy sharpening my oyster knife.

—Zora Neale Hurston

It's Finger-Lickin'-
Fuckin' Good.

—Kentucky Fried Chicken

Fucking less is fucking more.

—Robert Browning

Stay the fuck alive
all your fucking life.

—Norman Vincent Peale

Reader, I fucking married him.

—Charlotte Brontë

Everybody wants
to be Cary Grant.
Even I want to be
fucking Cary Grant.

—Cary Grant

Good night, and good fucking luck.

—Edward R. Murrow

Why the fuck does the universe go to all the bother of existing?

—Stephen Hawking

We are all in the gutter, but some of us are looking at the fucking stars.

—Oscar Wilde

A woman is like
a teabag—only in
hot fucking water
do you realize
how strong she is.

—Nancy Reagan

Give a hoot—
don't fuckin' pollute!

—Woodsy Owl, US Forest Service mascot

What the fuck do wom

—Sigmund Freud

want?

Whatever you can do,
or dream you can do,
begin it. Boldness has
fucking genius, power,
and magic in it!

—Johann Wolfgang von Goethe

The top of my head came off, and birds flew out, and the light changed, and I owned the city, and I knew why the fuck I was alive.

—Jane Fonda

I think your whole life shows in your face and you should be **fucking** proud of that.

—Lauren Bacall

Beef. It's what's for fucking dinner.

—National Cattlemen's Beef Association

Albums, like books and black lives, still fucking matter.

—Prince

All you fucking need is love.

—The Beatles

Fuckin' Rosebud.

—Charles Foster Kane, *Citizen Kane*